SO MANY QUESTIONS about... ANIMALS

Sally Spray and Mark Ruffle

WAYLAND
www.waylandbooks.co.uk

First published in Great Britain in 2022 by Wayland
© Hodder and Stoughton Limited, 2022

HB ISBN: 978 1 5263 1771 1
PB ISBN: 978 1 5263 1774 2

Editor: Paul Rockett
Design and illustration: Mark Ruffle
www.rufflebrothers.com

FSC
www.fsc.org

MIX
Paper from
responsible sources
FSC® C104740

Printed in Dubai

Wayland
An imprint of Hachette Children's Group
Part of Hodder & Stoughton
Carmelite House
50 Victoria Embankment
London EC4Y 0DZ

An Hachette UK Company
www.hachette.co.uk
www.hachettechildrens.co.uk

0422

Have you ever wanted to know about animals?
Think of all the questions you could ask ...

	Page
What are animals?	4
What do animals eat?	6
How do animals move?	8
What is the fastest animal?	10
How do animals have babies?	12
Why are animals different colours?	14
Which is the biggest animal?	16
Can animals survive in heat and cold?	18
What's the cutest animal or the scariest?	20
Which animals come out at night?	22
What is the rarest animal?	24
What is the future for animals?	26

I have lots of questions for you.

I can help! Let's take one question at a time and see what answers we can find.

Many more questions!	28	Game cards	30
Further information	28	Index	32
Glossary	29		

What are animals?

Animals

There are about 60,000 **vertebrate** species. All vertebrates have a backbone.

Warm-blooded

Cold-blooded

Mammals
have warm blood, hair and breathe air using their lungs. They give birth to live young and feed them with milk.

Elephant

Gorilla

Birds
have two legs, wings and feathers. Most can fly. The young hatch from eggs.

Scarlet macaw

Chicken

Fish
live in water, have gills to breathe and fins to swim. The young hatch from eggs.

Pufferfish

Paedocypris fish

Reptiles
breathe air with their lungs, have dry, scaly skin and lay eggs on land.

Nile crocodile

Leaf-tailed gecko

Amphibians
have moist skin and can live on land or in water. The young hatch from eggs, have gills when young and lungs when an adult.

Red-eyed tree frog

Poison dart frog

Think about ... how we organise animals into groups.

4

Animals are all the different creatures in the world. There are so many animals that it's useful to put them into groups, such as species, that classify their similarities and differences. Scientists have recorded almost 2 million different species of animal so far. They know there are many millions more yet to be discovered.

Below are some of the groups we put animals into.

There are about 1.25 million **invertebrate** species. Invertebrates don't have a backbone.

Insects
have six legs and a hard outer body in three sections. They lay eggs.

Mosquito

Ladybird

Arachnids
have eight legs and a hard two-part body. Their young hatch from eggs.

Red-kneed tarantula

Bird-dropping spider

Annelids
are segmented worms. They reproduce on their own.

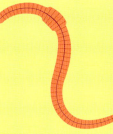

Earthworm

Leech

Crustaceans
have a hard shell and several pairs of jointed legs. The young hatch from eggs.

Red crab

Shrimp

Molluscs
have soft bodies and some have shells. They're found on land and in water, and lay eggs.

Garden snail

Giant Pacific octopus

Echinoderms
live in the sea. They have spiny skin and a circular symmetrical body.

Blue starfish

Sea urchin

Which group do whales belong to?
Which group do you belong to?

What must all animals do to stay alive?
Which animal do you want to learn about?

What do animals eat?

It depends on the kind of animal.

Herbivores mainly eat plants. I eat bamboo.

Omnivores eat plants and animals. A chimpanzee is an omnivore.

Carnivores, including lions and eagles, mainly eat animals.

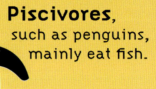

Piscivores, such as penguins, mainly eat fish.

Food chains show how plants and animals get their energy to live. Food chains always start with a producer, a plant that makes its own food from sunlight, water and nutrients. Producers are eaten by consumers. Consumers are prey for larger animals called predators.

Grass → Antelope → Lion → Scavengers — vulture

Plant → Earthworm → Bird → Fox

When animals and plants die, they start to break down. Eventually this releases nutrients into the soil, helping plants to grow.

Think about ... how energy passes along a food chain.

Lots of animals eat more than one thing, so they are part of many food chains. Together, the food chains make up a **food web**. If one animal or plant disappears from this pond food web, it will affect all the living things in the pond.

Biodiversity describes all the plants, trees and animals that live on Earth. A biodiverse planet has places for a huge variety of animals to live and food for them to eat. Humans present the biggest threat to Earth's biodiversity. Humans are destroying rainforests, over-fishing in the sea, building over the countryside and destroying wild places to grow crops.

Are you an omnivore, a herbivore or something else? Can you draw your own animal food chain?

Look at the pond on this page. Which animals and plants are linked together by what eats what?

How do animals move?

In so many different ways! Animals need to move to find food, escape from predators and find shelter or a mate. Look at these different animals on the move.

Most birds can **fly**. They have a light skeleton and long flight feathers. **Bats** are the only flying mammal.

Monkeys **climb** trees using their tail as an extra limb. Mountain goats in Morocco climb trees to eat the fruit!

We think of most mammals as having four legs to walk, run or jump like the springbok. But some mammals, including the kangaroo rat, **hop** around on two legs.

Ostriches cannot fly but they have powerful legs for **running**.

Think about ... the different ways animals move.

Penguins **waddle** or slide across snow. In the water their flippers and feet make them speedy swimmers.

A snake uses its muscular body and scales to grip the ground, travelling in a **winding, wavy motion.**

Moles use their large front paws to **burrow** through soil, chasing after earthworms.

A shark moves its tail and body from **side to side**, to power it through water.

Some animals travel incredible distances, usually to find food or to breed.

Arctic terns fly around 71,000 km a year, travelling from Greenland to Antarctica, via Africa and South America.

Humpback whales swim between Costa Rica and Antarctica, a journey of around 8,299 km.

Eels hatch in the Sargasso Sea. Then they drift and swim to rivers and lakes to grow into adults, before returning to the sea to lay eggs.

What other ways can animals move? How are an ostrich and a penguin similar or different?

Which animals can swim as well as run? How would it feel if you could fly?

What is the fastest animal?

Many animals have to move fast to catch their food or to prevent themselves from becoming another animal's dinner! Most animals can't keep up their top speed for long.

Scientists have found that medium-sized animals are the quickest. The ideal weight for animals that run or swim is 100 kg.

Thomson's gazelle can zig-zag, turn and jump to tire out a chasing cheetah, but sometimes the cheetah catches it.

The **cheetah** is the fastest land mammal, reaching speeds of 120.7 km/h. It can cover 7 m in a single bound.

The **peregrine falcon** can dive down on its prey at an astonishing 389 km/h.

The **white-throated needletail** flies at 171 km/h.

Think about ... the fastest and slowest animals.

The **fastest human** can run at 36 km/h over short distances.

The **sailfish** speeds through the water at speeds up to 110 km/h.

The **garden snail** moves slowly, sliding along on a trail of mucus it makes inside its body.

The fastest insect is an **Australian tiger beetle**, running at speeds up to 6.8 km/h.

The **manatee** floats between patches of seagrass and has no predators, so it doesn't need to swim above 8 km/h.

The **three-toed sloth** moves very slowly. At its fastest it only moves 0.27 km/h.

What are the advantages and disadvantages of being a fast or a slow animal?

Which animals could you outrun? When do you move quickly or slowly?

How do animals have babies?

Almost all animals need a male and a female to reproduce, creating baby animals. Some hatch from eggs, others are born. Many young animals look after themselves from the start while others need their parents' care.

Birds and reptiles lay eggs, from which their babies hatch. Turtles hatch on their own. Birds keep their eggs warm and feed their chicks when they hatch.

The female **seahorse** lays her eggs in her mate's pouch. He looks after them until they hatch.

Baby mammals grow inside their mother. Once they are born, their mother feeds them with her milk until her young can find food for themselves.

A rabbit can have between one and 14 rabbits in one litter.

Marsupials are mammals. Once they are born, the tiny babies crawl into their mother's pouch and stay there to feed and grow.

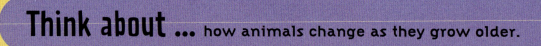

Think about ... how animals change as they grow older.

Baby animals become adults in different ways.
Some change more than others.

Butterflies and moths lay their eggs on leaves. Hungry caterpillars hatch out and eat to grow. Eventually, they form a hard case called a pupa. Inside the pupa the caterpillar transforms into an adult which can fly, feed and reproduce.

Most frogs lay masses of eggs, called spawn, in water. They hatch into young wriggly tadpoles which swim, eat and grow, breathing through gills. Gradually they develop lungs, grow legs, lose their tails and become adult hopping frogs.

Eggs

Spawn

Adult frog

Tadpole

Baby elephants are born looking very like their parents. They can walk within hours. The mother cares for her young but the whole herd helps out.

Which of the animals on this page gives birth to live young? Which animals do you think make the best parents?

How different are chicks to adult birds? How have you changed since you were born?

13

Why are animals different colours?

An animal's colouring can help it survive. It can help it attract a mate or hide from predators. It can even scare predators away!

Can you find three animals hiding in this tree? Their colours act as a **camouflage** to help them blend into their surroundings.

The **eyed-hawk moth** uses the eyespots on its wings to trick a predator into thinking the moth is a bigger, more fierce creature than it is.

Think about ... the different ways animals use camouflage.

14

The colours of the harmless **scarlet kingsnake** mimic those of the deadly coral snake.

The **hornet moth** looks like a dangerous stinging hornet. This keeps predators away.

To stop birds eating them, the **bird-dropping spider** looks like a bird poo!

Chameleons and **octopuses** can change their colours in a flash! They do this to hide, to communicate or warn others of their mood.

Poisonous frogs are brightly coloured to both attract mates and to warn other animals not to eat them.

Ladybirds' bright colours warn predators of their bitter taste.

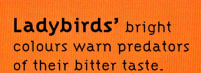

The showy **peacock** swishes its colourful tail feathers around to attract a mate.

The male **magnificent frigatebird** can inflate his red throat like a giant red balloon to impress the females.

Which animal on these pages is the hardest to spot? Why are male birds usually more colourful than females?

What other animals can you think of that mimic more dangerous animals?

Which is the biggest animal?

The blue whale is the largest animal ever to have lived. Blue whales can grow to over 30 m long — the length of a basketball court!

The **colossal squid** is 12-14 m long and has eyes as big as beach balls. It lives deep underwater in the oceans around Antarctica.

African elephants are the largest land mammals, weighing as much as 6,350 kg. They feed on plants for around 16 hours per day.

The **giant weta** is the heaviest insect, at 70 g. It looks like a cricket but is too heavy to jump.

Think about ... why animals come in all shapes and sizes.

These are the smallest animals.
They'd all fit in your hand.

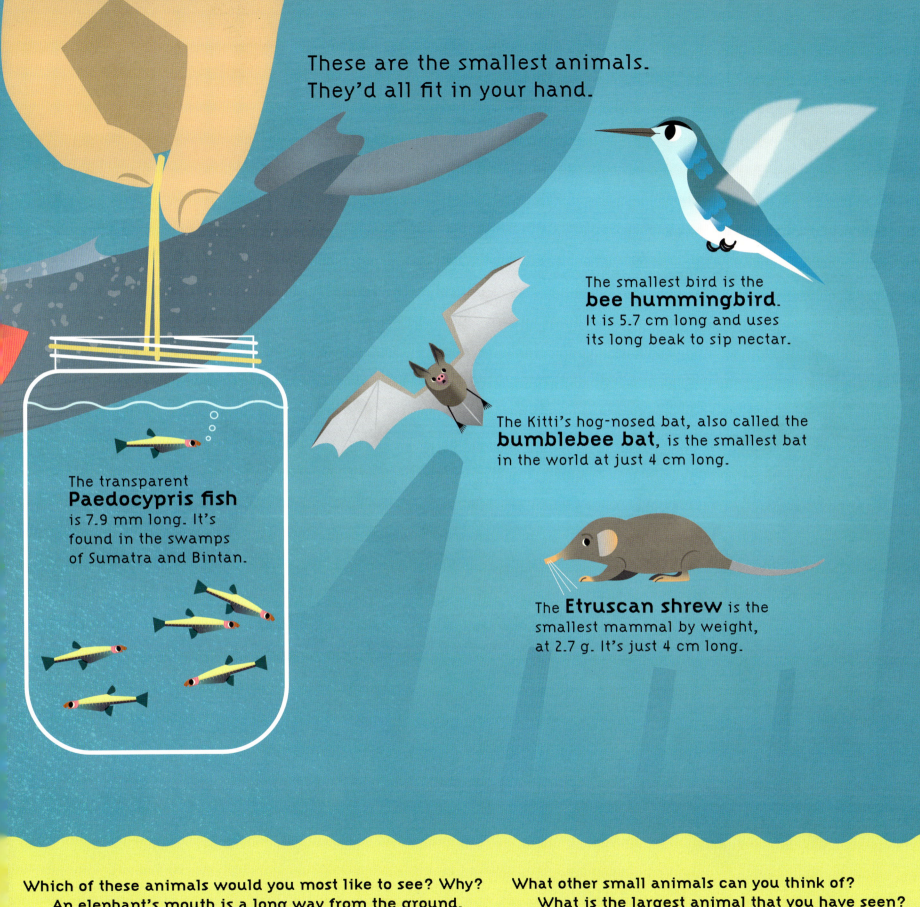

The smallest bird is the
bee hummingbird.
It is 5.7 cm long and uses
its long beak to sip nectar.

The Kitti's hog-nosed bat, also called the
bumblebee bat, is the smallest bat
in the world at just 4 cm long.

The transparent
Paedocypris fish
is 7.9 mm long. It's
found in the swamps
of Sumatra and Bintan.

The **Etruscan shrew** is the
smallest mammal by weight,
at 2.7 g. It's just 4 cm long.

Which of these animals would you most like to see? Why?
An elephant's mouth is a long way from the ground.
What helps it feed and drink?

What other small animals can you think of?
What is the largest animal that you have seen?

Can animals survive in heat and cold?

Yes! Some animals are perfectly adapted for living in very hot or cold places.

The **emperor penguin** lives in Antarctica, the coldest place on Earth. It has two layers of feathers and a layer of fat to keep it warm.

The **Arctic fox** has thick fur to help it survive the extreme cold. Its fur changes colour with the seasons, from brown in the summer to white in winter to match the landscape.

Polar bears live in the Arctic Circle. They can swim in the freezing waters for days at a time without stopping, kept warm by a layer of fat under their skin called blubber.

Think about ... how some animals are able to live in cold places.

Dromedaries, also called Arabian camels, have several adaptations for life in the desert.

Its **eyes** are protected from sand by two rows of eyelashes.

Its **hump** stores fat so it can survive long periods without food.

Its wide **feet** feet stop it from sinking into sand.

Silver desert ants have shiny, reflective skin to protect them from the heat of the midday Sun. They hunt for 10 minutes at a time, attacking other insects that are suffering from heatstroke.

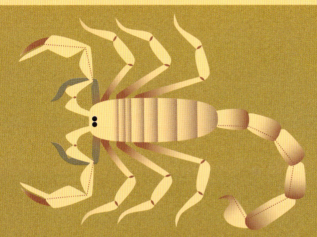

Scorpions burrow beneath the hot desert sand to stay cool. They nip out to kill their prey with their tail sting.

How about living in the intestines of other animals? It's where **parasitic tapeworms** live, hanging on using suckers and hooks. They can live inside all sorts of animals, from deer to dolphins. Inside whales they can grow to be 30 m long!

How else do different animals adapt to living in very hot places?

Which reptiles live in deserts?
What can you find out about other parasites?

What's the cutest animal or the scariest?

The answer to this question varies from person to person! I think all these animals are cute. They're all furry and look nice to cuddle, although the lion cub's dad doesn't look so friendly!

I prefer brightly coloured animals, like the red-eyed tree frog, the red-kneed tarantula, the San Francisco garter snake and the jewel wasp.

Think about ... how you react to different sorts of animal.

Some people are afraid of certain animals, especially snakes and spiders. There are special words for the fear felt by some people towards groups of animals.

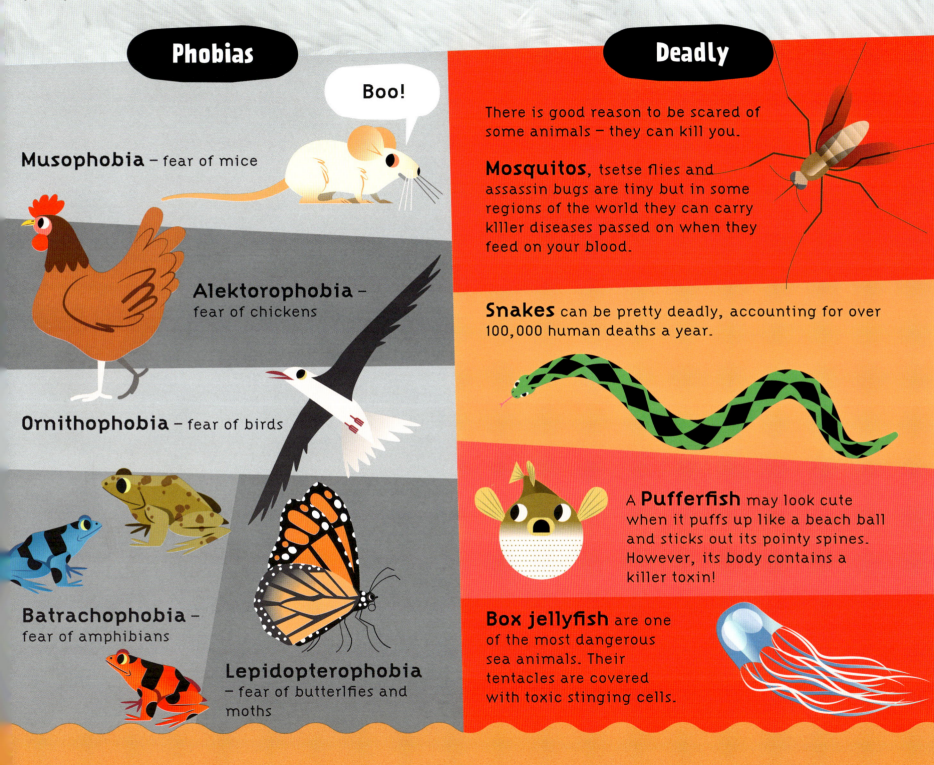

Phobias

Boo!

Musophobia – fear of mice

Alektorophobia – fear of chickens

Ornithophobia – fear of birds

Batrachophobia – fear of amphibians

Lepidopterophobia – fear of butterlfies and moths

Deadly

There is good reason to be scared of some animals – they can kill you.

Mosquitos, tsetse flies and assassin bugs are tiny but in some regions of the world they can carry killer diseases passed on when they feed on your blood.

Snakes can be pretty deadly, accounting for over 100,000 human deaths a year.

A **Pufferfish** may look cute when it puffs up like a beach ball and sticks out its pointy spines. However, its body contains a killer toxin!

Box jellyfish are one of the most dangerous sea animals. Their tentacles are covered with toxic stinging cells.

Which of these animals do you find cute or scary? What makes you scared of an animal?

Cute or scary, all animals are important. Can you explain why?

21

Which animals come out at night?

As the Sun sets and the Moon starts to shine, nocturnal creatures come out to hunt. It's cooler at night and easier for animals to hide. Many predators have big eyes and amazing hearing or they use echo location to help them find food.

Bats find flying insects by making sounds which bounce off their prey back to the bat's ears, letting it place objects around it.

An **owl** silently swoops through the night, hunting for insects and rodents, relying on sensitive hearing and sight. They can catch prey in flight and even snatch them from out of the water.

Think about ... what the world is like at night.

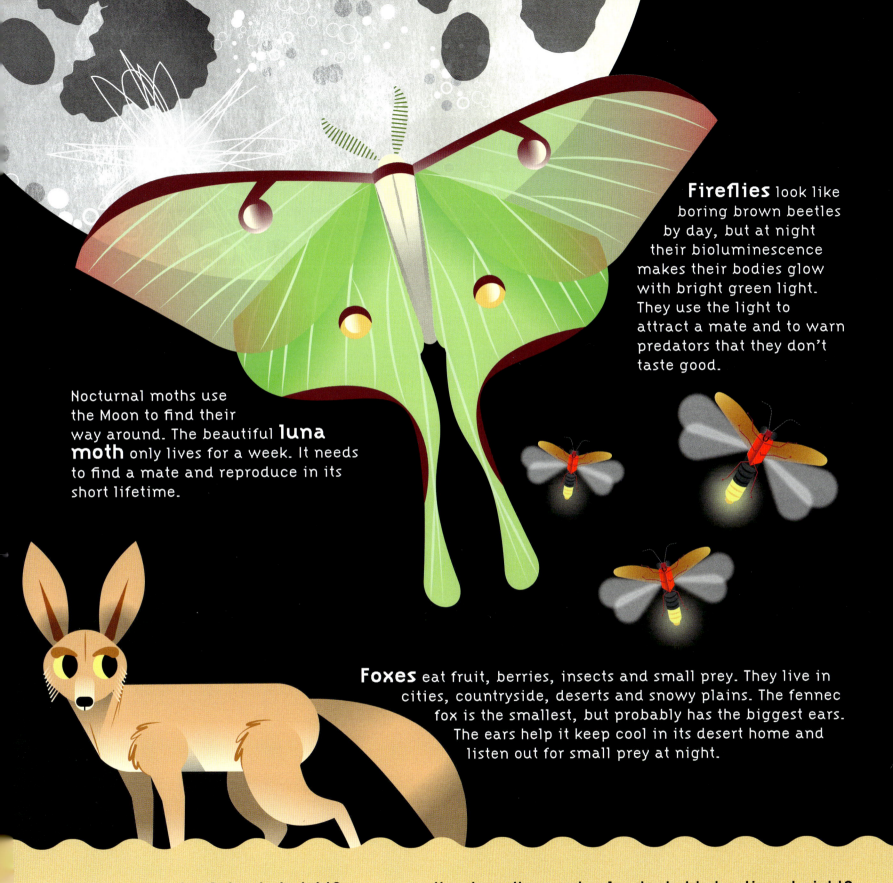

Fireflies look like boring brown beetles by day, but at night their bioluminescence makes their bodies glow with bright green light. They use the light to attract a mate and to warn predators that they don't taste good.

Nocturnal moths use the Moon to find their way around. The beautiful **luna moth** only lives for a week. It needs to find a mate and reproduce in its short lifetime.

Foxes eat fruit, berries, insects and small prey. They live in cities, countryside, deserts and snowy plains. The fennec fox is the smallest, but probably has the biggest ears. The ears help it keep cool in its desert home and listen out for small prey at night.

Why do some animals hunt at night?
When do nocturnal hunters sleep?

How have these animals adapted to hunting at night?
Have you seen any of these nocturnal animals?
Which ones?

23

What is the rarest animal?

The vaquita is probably the rarest animal in the world. Check it out at the bottom of this page. Sadly, the total number of animals worldwide has declined by over half in the last 50 years. Some of these amazing animals may disappear altogether.

Conservationists are working hard to keep the world's rarest bird, the **Madagascar pochard duck**, from dying out. There are less than 50 left.

Rhinos are hunted for their horns and their habitat is being destroyed. There are only 27,000 left. The western black rhino and northern white rhino are already extinct.

The **purple frog** lives most of its life underground, so it's hard to count these rare amphibians. They only emerge for a few days a year to find a mate.

The **vaquita** is the smallest member of the whale family. They die in fishing nets meant for fish. There may only be 10 left.

Think about ... how we can help protect endangered animals.

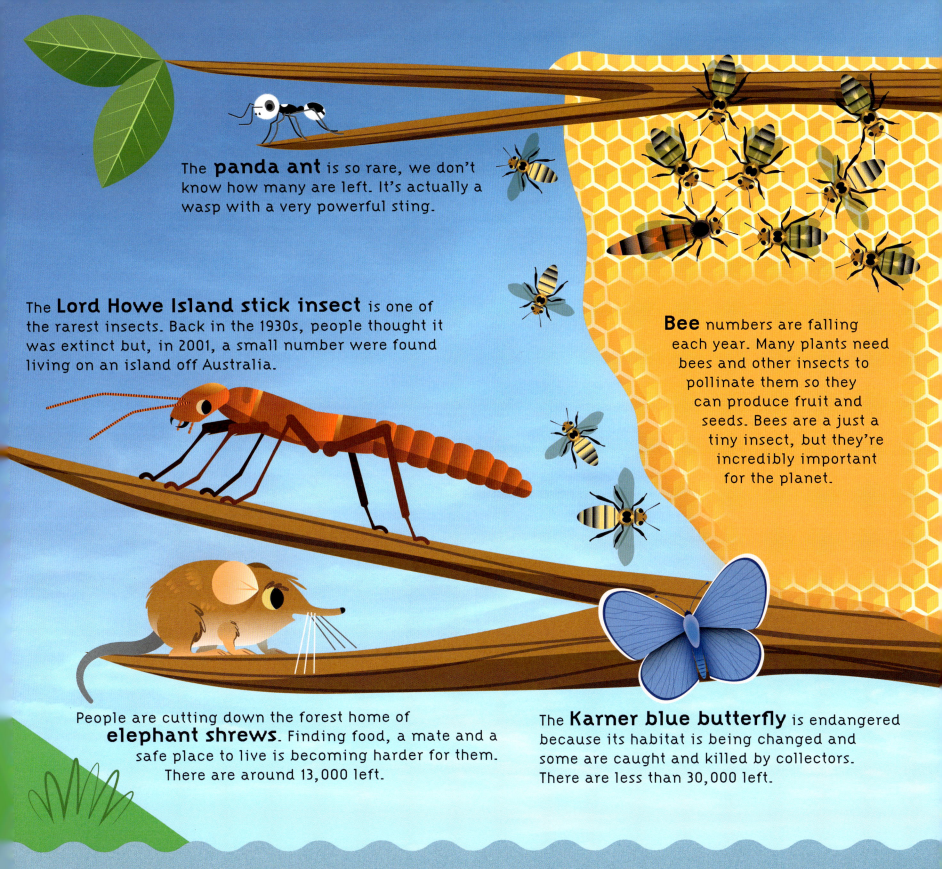

The **panda ant** is so rare, we don't know how many are left. It's actually a wasp with a very powerful sting.

The **Lord Howe Island stick insect** is one of the rarest insects. Back in the 1930s, people thought it was extinct but, in 2001, a small number were found living on an island off Australia.

Bee numbers are falling each year. Many plants need bees and other insects to pollinate them so they can produce fruit and seeds. Bees are a just a tiny insect, but they're incredibly important for the planet.

People are cutting down the forest home of **elephant shrews**. Finding food, a mate and a safe place to live is becoming harder for them. There are around 13,000 left.

The **Karner blue butterfly** is endangered because its habitat is being changed and some are caught and killed by collectors. There are less than 30,000 left.

What causes an animal to become endangered? How are people responsible?

What would happen if bees and insects died out? What could you do to help protect them?

Educate
Find out about animals and pass your knowledge on.

What is the future for animals?

Thousands of animals are in danger of becoming extinct. Let's think about how we can all help to protect animals.

Support
Support organisations that help animals in the wild or protect species in zoos.

SAVE THE WHALE

DON'T WEAR FUR

Think about ... what you'd like the future to be like for animals.

Protect

Protect their habitats and make your space wildlife-friendly.

Eat less meat

Eat less meat and ask for free-range, organic or high welfare foods.

Pets

Look after your pets. Exercise them, feed them the right foods and care for them well.

Observe

Try to observe animals to learn from them. Think about and appreciate their importance.

It's over to you. The future survival of animals is in your hands. Why is it important to protect animals and their habitats?

Many more questions!

1. What are arachnids?

2. What is faster, the cheetah or the peregrine falcon?

3. Which new animal have you discovered in this book?

4. Can you name three animals that hop?

5. How does the hornet moth mimic a hornet?

6. Why are some animals endangered?

7. How many tentacles does a colossal squid have? And how many arms?

8. Which is the deadliest animal?

9. Are you scared of any animals? Why don't you like them?

10. What animal would you like to be and why?

Further information

Websites

www.animalfactguide.com

www.natgeokids.com

wwf.panda.org

Books

Darwin's Tree of Life by Michael Bright (Wayland, 2019)

Discover and Do: Animals by Jane Lacey (Franklin Watts, 2021)

Quick Fix Science: Animals by Paul Mason (Wayland, 2021)

Glossary

Adaptation – a special feature that helps a living thing to survive. Adaptations pass from a living thing to its offspring

Bioluminescence – the ability to make light within an animal's body

Classify – sort into groups with similar features

Colossal – very large, huge

Conservationist – someone who works to protect wildlife and the environment

Drought – a long period of time without any rainfall

Echolocation – when an animal makes a sound and listens for the returning echo sound in order to work out where objects are around it

Endangered – at risk of dying out and becoming extinct

Extinct – when a living thing dies out completely, leaving none of that species alive

Food chain – the plants and animals linked together by what eats what

Food web – the food chains linked together by what eats what in a habitat

Free-range – farm animals raised with enough space to move about and feed

Gills – special parts of a fish or young amphibian on either side of its head, used for breathing

Habitat – the place where a plant or animal normally lives

High-welfare – farm animals reared with good access to space, clean water, fresh air and good food

Invertebrate – one of a huge group of animals without a backbone

Litter – young born to the same mother at the same time

Marsupial – a group of mammals that carry their young in a pouch. Kangaroos, koalas and opossums are all marsupials

Mimic – to look or behave like someone or something else

Mucus – a slimy liquid produced by animals such as snails and slugs

Nocturnal – active at night

Nutrient – something used by a living thing as food to live and grow

Organic – food grown without the use of artificial chemicals

Parasitic – an animal and plant that lives on or inside another animal or plant and gets its food from it

Phobia – a very strong fear of something

Pollinate – to move pollen from one flower to another, leading to fertilisation. It allows a plant to make fruit and seeds

Predator – an animal that hunts and eats other animals

Prey – an animal that is hunted by another animal for food

Reflective – bouncing back light

Reproduce – when animals reproduce, they have young

Rodent – a mammal with big teeth. Rats, squirrels, mice and guinea pigs are all rodents

Scavenger – an animal that feeds on dead animals or dead plants

Species – a kind of living thing, such as a luna moth

Symmetrical – when something is the same shape and size on both sides

Tentacle – a long, thin part of an animal's body used for feeling, grabbing or holding things.

Toxic – poisonous

Transparent – a material that you can see through clearly

Venomous – an animal with a poisonous sting or bite

Vertebrate – one of a huge number of animals with a backbone

Game cards

You can play with the game cards in a number of ways:
Choose an animal card and get a friend to ask questions that you can answer with a yes or no,
e.g. Does it have wings?
They can guess the animal card through a process of elimination.

Name Elephant
Description
It's got a trunk!

Length 650 cm
Fins or limbs 4
Lifespan Up to 70 years
Number of teeth 26

Name Red-kneed
tarantula
Description
It's got 8 eyes!

Length 20 cm
Fins or limbs 8
Lifespan Up to 30 years
Number of teeth 0

Name Lion
Description
King of the Jungle

Length 300 cm
Fins or limbs 4
Lifespan Up to 14 years
Number of teeth 30

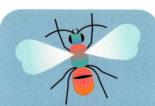

Name Jewel wasp
Description
Tiny, shiny wasp

Length 2 cm
Fins or limbs 6
Lifespan Up to 1 year
Number of teeth 0

Name Octopus
Description
Clever cephlapod

Length 1.3 m
Fins or limbs 8
Lifespan Up to 5 years
Number of teeth 0

Name Karner blue
butterfly
Description
Rare blue butterfly

Length 2.5 cm
Fins or limbs 6
Lifespan Up to 5 days
Number of teeth 0

Name Elephant shrew
Description
Rare mammal

Length 30 cm
Fins or limbs 4
Lifespan Up to 4 years
Number of teeth 44

Name Dromedary
Description
One hump

Length 341 cm
Fins or limbs 4
Lifespan Up to 40 years
Number of teeth 32

Name Barn owl
Description
Night hunter

Length 40 cm
Fins or limbs 4
Lifespan Up to 25 years
Number of teeth 0

Name Poison dart frog
Description
Bright, toxic frog

Length 6 cm
Fins or limbs 4
Lifespan Up to 20 years
Number of teeth 0

Name Mosquito
Description
Buzzy bloodsucker

Length 1 cm
Fins or limbs 6
Lifespan Up to 7 days
Number of teeth 0

Name Luna moth
Description
Moonlight moth

Length 11.5 cm
Fins or limbs 6
Lifespan Up to 7 days
Number of teeth 0

Name Ostrich
Description
Can run at 70 km/h

Length 270 cm
Fins or limbs 4
Lifespan Up to 40 years
Number of teeth 0

Name Pipistrelle bat
Description
Big-eared bug hunter

Length 4 cm
Fins or limbs 4
Lifespan Up to 5 years
Number of teeth 17

Name Pufferfish
Description
Inflatable fish!

Length Up to 61 cm
Fins or limbs 5
Lifespan Up to 10 years
Number of teeth 4

Photograph or scan the cards, print them, cut them out and you can play the following games:
- Top Trumps
- Snap (you will need to print out two sets of cards)
- Lotto (you will need to print out two sets of cards)
- Matching pairs (you will need to print out two sets of cards).

Create your own animal cards to add to the pack!

Name Arctic tern
Description
Flies 35,000 km a year

Length 41 cm
Fins or limbs 4
Lifespan Up to 30 years
Number of teeth 0

Name Farm bird
Description
Egg laying beauty

Length 40 cm
Fins or limbs 4
Lifespan Up to 10 years
Number of teeth 0

Name Honeybee
Description
Honey-maker

Length 1.5 cm
Fins or limbs 6
Lifespan Up to 28 days
Number of teeth 0

Name Standard poodle
Description
Clever and cute

Length 81 cm
Fins or limbs 4
Lifespan Up to 15 years
Number of teeth 42

Name Panda ant
Description
Wingless wasp

Length 0.8 cm
Fins or limbs 6
Lifespan Up to 2 years
Number of teeth 0

Name Thick-tailed scorpion
Description
It's a stinger!

Length 14 cm
Fins or limbs 8
Lifespan Up to 5 years
Number of teeth 0

Name Emperor penguin
Description
Largest penguin

Length 120 cm
Fins or limbs 4
Lifespan Up to 20 years
Number of teeth 0

Name Christmas Island red crab
Description
Merry Christmas crab

Length 11 cm
Fins or limbs 10
Lifespan Up to 30 years
Number of teeth 3

Name Jerboa
Description
Happy hoppy rodent

Length 15 cm
Fins or limbs 4
Lifespan Up to 5 years
Number of teeth 16

Name Frigatebird
Description
Red balloon chest

Length 100 cm
Fins or limbs 4
Lifespan Up to 25 years
Number of teeth 0

Name Garden snail
Description
Slime slider

Length 3 cm
Fins or limbs 1
Lifespan Up to 5 years
Number of teeth 14,000

Name Blue whale
Description
Largest animal in the world

Length 2,900 cm
Fins or limbs 4
Lifespan Up to 90 years
Number of teeth 0

Name Firefly
Description
It glows at night

Length 2.5 cm
Fins or limbs 6
Lifespan Up to 2 years
Number of teeth 0

Name Springbok
Description
Jumping antelope

Length 200 cm
Fins or limbs 4
Lifespan Up to 9 years
Number of teeth 28

Name Giant panda
Description
Black and white bear

Length 190 cm
Fins or limbs 4
Lifespan Up to 20 years
Number of teeth 42

Index

amphibians 4, 21
 frogs 4–5, 13, 15, 20, 24
animals
 adaptations to heat and cold 18–19
 camouflage and colour 14–15
 classification 4–5
 diet 6–7
 endangered 24–26
 mimicry 15
 movement 8–11
 nocturnal 22–23
 poisonous 21
 reproduction 4–5, 12–13, 23
 size 16–17
annelids 5
 earthworms 5–6, 9
 tapeworms 19
arachnids 5, 21
 bird-dropping spiders 5, 15
 red-kneed tarantulas 5, 20
 scorpions 19

biodiversity 7
birds 4, 6, 8, 12–13, 15, 21
 Arctic terns 9
 bee hummingbirds 17
 chickens 4, 20–21
 eagles 6
 Madagascar pochard duck 24
 magnificent frigatebirds 15
 ostriches 8–9
 owls 22
 peacocks 15
 penguins 6, 9, 18
 peregrine falcons 10
 scarlet macaws 4
 vultures 6
 white-throated needletail 10

carnivores 6
consumers 6
crustaceans 5
 red crab 5
 shrimps 5

echinoderms 5
 box jellyfish 21
 sea urchins 5
 starfish 5
echolocation 22

fish 4, 6, 9
 eels 9
 Paedocypris fish 4, 17
 pufferfish 4, 21
 sailfish 11
 seahorses 12
 sharks 9
food chains 6–7
food webs 7

habitat destruction 7, 24–25
herbivores 6–7

insects 5, 22, 25
 ants 19, 25
 Australian tiger beetle 11
 bees 25
 butterflies 13, 21, 25
 fireflies 23
 giant wetas 16
 jewel wasps 20
 ladybirds 5, 15
 Lord Howe Island stick insects 25
 mosquitos 5, 21
 moths 13–15, 21, 23

mammals 4, 12, 21
 antelopes 6
 bats 8, 17, 22
 cheetahs 10
 chimpanzees 6
 dogs 20

dromedaries 19
elephant shrews 25
elephants 4, 13, 16–17
Etruscan shrews 17
foxes 6, 18, 23
goats 8
gorillas 4
kangaroo rats 8
lions 6, 20
manatees 11
marsupials 12
moles 9
monkeys 8
polar bears 18
rabbits 12, 20
rhinos 24
springboks 8
Thomson's gazelles 10
three-toed sloths 11
vaquitas 24
whales 5, 9, 16, 19
molluscs 5
 colossal squids 16
 octopuses 5, 15
 snails 5, 11

omnivores 6–7

parasites 19
phobias 21
piscivores 6
predators 6, 8, 10–11, 14, 22–23
producers 6

reptiles 4, 12, 19
 chameleon 15
 leaf-tailed geckos 4
 Nile crocodiles 4
 snakes 9, 15, 20–21
 turtles 12

scavengers 6